BASEBALL

AND ITS GREATEST PLAYERS

in**side** *sports*

BASEBALL

AND ITS GREATEST PLAYERS

EDITED BY MICHAEL ANDERSON

Britannica®
Educational Publishing
IN ASSOCIATION WITH

ROSEN
EDUCATIONAL SERVICES

Published in 2012 by Britannica Educational Publishing
(a trademark of Encyclopædia Britannica, Inc.)
in association with Rosen Educational Services, LLC
29 East 21st Street, New York, NY 10010.

Distributed exclusively by Rosen Educational Services.
For a listing of additional Britannica Educational Publishing titles, call toll free (800) 237-9932.

First Edition

Britannica Educational Publishing
Michael I. Levy: Executive Editor, Encyclopædia Britannica
J.E. Luebering: Director, Core Reference Group, Encyclopædia Britannica
Adam Augustyn: Assistant Manager, Encyclopædia Britannica

Anthony L. Green: Editor, Compton's by Britannica
Michael Anderson: Senior Editor, Compton's by Britannica
Sherman Hollar: Associate Editor, Compton's by Britannica

Marilyn L. Barton: Senior Coordinator, Production Control
Steven Bosco: Director, Editorial Technologies
Lisa S. Braucher: Senior Producer and Data Editor
Yvette Charboneau: Senior Copy Editor
Kathy Nakamura: Manager, Media Acquisition

Rosen Educational Services
Hope Lourie Killcoyne: Senior Editor and Project Manager
Nelson Sá: Art Director
Cindy Reiman: Photography Manager
Matthew Cauli: Designer, Cover Design
Introduction by Hope Lourie Killcoyne

Library of Congress Cataloging-in-Publication Data

Baseball and its greatest players / edited by Michael Anderson.
    p. cm.—(Inside sports)
"In association with Britannica Educational Publishing, Rosen Educational Services."
Includes bibliographical references and index.
ISBN 978-1-61530-510-0 (library binding)
1. Baseball—United States--History. 2. Baseball players—United States—History. I. Anderson,
Michael (Michael J.), 1972-
GV863.A1.B37645 2010
796.357'640973—dc22

                                                                        2010052806

Manufactured in the United States of America

On the cover, page 3: First baseman Albert Pujols of the St. Louis Cardinals bats during an away
game against the Los Angeles Dodgers in 2005. After that season, having hit .330 with 41 homers and
117 runs batted in, Pujols was named the National League's Most Valuable Player. *Stephen Dunn/Getty
Images*

Pages 6,7, 88, 90, 93, 94 © www.istockphoto.com/Willie B. Thomas; pp 10, 24, 43, 56, 66, 86 ©www.
istockphoto.com/Steven Hendricks; pp. 14, 15, 20, 48 © www.istockphoto.com/stock_art; back cover,
remaining interior background image Shutterstock.com

CONTENTS

INTRODUCTION

Think about baseball for a moment. What comes to mind? Childhood experiences from Little League, such as the thrill of sliding into home plate or the anguish of being tagged out on second? Staying up late to watch a game on TV with friends and family? Going to see a game in person, with the sharp shouts of souvenir vendors, the crisp crack of the bat, and the crowd's cheers and chants?

Around the world, and especially for many in America, there is a deep and emotional component to the game. As former baseball commissioner A. Bartlett "Bart" Giamatti said in his essay "Green Fields of the Mind": "It breaks your heart. It is designed to break your heart. The game begins in the spring, when everything else begins again, and it blossoms in the summer, filling the afternoons and evenings, and then as soon as the chill rains come, it stops and leaves you to face the fall alone."

Though by numbers alone baseball players, managers, and owners represent but a small facet of society—and a male-dominated facet at that—the influence of the game extends far beyond the diamond. In the United States, where baseball has long occupied a special place in the country's psyche, it has also served as a kind of national mirror. A country that prides itself on abiding by the rule of law, America and baseball have grown up together, guided by—and sometimes falling short of—the game's goals of good sportsmanship and fair play. An early example of a moral lapse occurred nearly a century ago, with the notorious game-fixing Black Sox Scandal of 1919. Happily, a few decades later, great strides forward were made as the issue of racial integration took center field, and Jackie Robinson broke the color barrier by joining the Brooklyn Dodgers in 1947. As for recent headlines, the rise of performance-enhancing drug use calls into question how far Americans are willing to go to see new records set. The staggering rise in salaries, too, has tested public goodwill

A ball arcing into the stands brings the game of baseball to a whole new level of excitement for fans. Here at Wrigley Field, spectators become participants as they scramble for the ball at a 2010 game between the Chicago Cubs and the Milwaukee Brewers. Chicago Tribune/McClatchy-Tribune/Getty Images

toward the sport. In the era of free agency, superstars can command salaries and endorsements of more than 30 million dollars a year. For some, the schism between player incomes and those of the average fan—national census figures show that the median household income for 2009 hovered at around 50 thousand dollars—reflects not only the excess of the sports world but also a country increasingly divided between rich and poor.

Going beyond America's shores, this book documents the global reach of the sport—in Latin America and Asia—because from Cuba to Korea, Venezuela to Japan, baseball has millions of fans around the world. But no matter where the game is played, baseball is perennially about personalities, statistics, and of course, athleticism. As this concise volume brings readers back to the game's origins, explaining the ins and outs of the sport, it also highlights luminaries from Hank Aaron to Ichiro Suzuki, exceptional players who have made baseball the game it is today.

Although baseball legend Yogi Berra, famous for his one-liners, said of the game, "In baseball you don't know nothing," *Baseball and Its Greatest Players* provides a brief but insightful look at the game so that readers, will indeed, come away knowing something.

9

CHAPTER 1

A WORLD SPORT WITH AMERICAN ORIGINS

The sport of baseball developed in the eastern United States in the mid-1800s. From there it spread to big cities and small towns across the country. By the turn of the 20th century, baseball was known as America's national pastime. To some people, baseball was also considered a symbol of the country's character. "Whoever wants to know the heart and mind of America had better learn baseball, the rules and realities of the game," wrote American author and historian Jacques Barzun.

The United States is not the only country where the game has had a large impact. Baseball is also a national passion in Cuba, Puerto Rico, the Dominican Republic, and Venezuela. And in Mexico, Japan, and Korea, baseball has thrived since the early 1900s. Whereas the United States can boast of legendary players such as Babe Ruth and Willie Mays, elsewhere fans praise the talents of baseball heroes such as Martin Dihigo of Cuba, Roberto Clemente of Puerto Rico, and Sadaharu Oh of Japan. Today, television, radio, print media, and Web sites provide information on players and teams for millions of baseball fans in all corners of the globe.

Baseball is played by two teams of nine players. On the inner part of the field are four white bases laid out in a square. The basic equipment consists of a bat, ball, and gloves. During a game, the two teams alternate between being fielders (playing defense) and batters (playing offense). The object of the game is to score more runs than the opponent. A run is scored each time a player on the offensive team is able to run to and touch all four bases. A period of play called an inning is completed when both teams have had a turn at bat. The team with the most runs after nine innings wins the game. If there is a tie, extra innings are played until a winner emerges.

NORTH AMERICA

The two major professional leagues in North America are the National League (NL)

and the American League (AL), which are governed by an organization called Major League Baseball. There are also professional minor league teams in many American cities. In addition, baseball is one of the more important amateur sports in the United States, with several well-organized leagues for youth and junior players, as well as a long-standing college tradition.

Major and Minor Leagues

For most of their early history, the National and American leagues each had eight teams, and every team played a 154-game schedule to determine the league champions. The league champions would then meet in the World Series. Currently the American League has 14 teams, and the National League has 16 teams. Each league is divided into Eastern, Central, and Western divisions, and each team plays 162 regular-season games. The team with the best record in each division at the end of the season is a division champion. In October, each of the division champions and two wild-card teams (the teams with the best record among the non–division-winning teams in each league) advance to

Pitcher Brian Wilson and his San Francisco Giants teammates celebrate the series-winning moment of the 2010 World Series. The Giants clinched the title on Nov. 1, 2010, in game five against the Texas Rangers. **Damian Strohmeyer/Sports Illustrated/Getty Images**

the play-offs. Best-of-five-games series are played in the first round. The winning teams from the first round move on to compete in a second-round, best-of-seven-games series to determine the league's champion, or pennant winner. The American League and National League pennant winners then play a best-of-seven-games World Series to determine the overall champion.

BASEBALL HALL OF FAME

In Cooperstown, N.Y., stands the National Baseball Hall of Fame and Museum. It was dedicated in 1939. The first members of the Hall of Fame had been chosen in 1936. They were Ty Cobb, Walter Johnson, Christy Mathewson, Babe Ruth, and Honus Wagner.

The legendary Babe Ruth, seen here at Yankee Stadium in the Bronx, New York City, shows a young fan how to hold a baseball bat. Hulton Archive/Getty Images

In an annual selection process, the members of the Baseball Writers' Association of America elect players for membership in the Hall of Fame. Eligible players must have been active within the previous 20 years, but not for the five years preceding the election. A special committee of baseball veterans selects players inactive for at least 21 years and managers and umpires inactive for at least five years. Another special committee elects players and other personnel, such as executives and owners, who were active in the Negro Leagues.

The midseason All-Star Game, contested between the most popular American League and National League players, began in 1933. Fans vote to select the starting lineups, and the team managers select pitchers and substitute players. Since 2003, the outcome of the All-Star Game has determined which league receives home-field advantage in the World Series.

Minor league teams are affiliated with specific major league teams and serve as training grounds for ballplayers with major league potential. The minor leagues are classified as AAA, AA, and A, according to the relative length of professional experience

of the players. The National Association of Professional Baseball Leagues governs the minor leagues.

LITTLE LEAGUE AND COLLEGE BASEBALL

The best-known youth baseball league is the Little League, which was founded in 1939 in Williamsport, Pa. Teams compete in more than 100 countries, and players aged 10–12 vie with each other for the opportunity to play in the Little League World Series. Little League Baseball now provides competitions for players ranging from ages 5 to 18. Other organized leagues include the Babe Ruth League and PONY (Protect Our Nation's Youth) Baseball, Inc. American Legion Baseball is for those 19 and under who play on a regulation diamond under regular baseball rules.

Baseball games between college teams have been played regularly since the American Civil War. National champions are determined in tournaments held by the National Collegiate Athletic Association (NCAA), the National Association of Intercollegiate Athletics, and the National Junior College Athletic Association.

Little League teams such as this one in New York City provide young players with the opportunity to learn the fundamentals of baseball.
Hope Lourie Killcoyne

LATIN AMERICA

Baseball arrived in Latin America in the 1860s. In Cuba, students returning home from studies in the United States introduced the game to their compatriots. The sport quickly spread throughout the island and became a national passion. In the late 1800s, Cubans were instrumental in introducing the game to the Dominican Republic and throughout the Caribbean region. Cubans, along with American railroad workers and merchant marine, took the game to Mexico, Venezuela, and Central America.

Cuba established a professional winter league in 1878. Professional baseball was played there until 1961. It was then restructured into an amateur competition by the communist government of Fidel Castro. Cubans continue to be very passionate about baseball. The amateur league has produced many fine players, and Cuba's Olympic baseball teams have won several gold medals. In order to play professional baseball in the United States, some of Cuba's best ballplayers, such as pitchers (and brothers) Orlando and Liván Hernández, have fled Cuba.

There are professional leagues in the Dominican Republic, Mexico, Puerto Rico,

The Hernández brothers are pictured in 1998 at Yankee Stadium. Once pitchers on the Cuban national team, Liván (left) defected from Cuba in 1995, while his older half-brother Orlando fled Cuba in 1997. Louis DeLuca/MLB Photos via Getty Images

INTERNATIONAL TOURNAMENTS

At the international level, baseball teams representing their countries have competed in various organized tournaments. Baseball has been an official medal sport at the Summer Olympic Games since 1992. (Unofficial exhibition games were played at the Olympics long before that, however.) Another international baseball event, a World Cup tournament, has been held since 1938. The International Baseball Federation organizes the World Cup and several other baseball competitions. The federation has a membership of more than 100 countries.

In 2006 a new international event known as the World Baseball Classic was held. Major League Baseball and the Major League Baseball Players Association established the tournament, which was contested between 16 national teams. The games were played in Japan, Puerto Rico, and the United States. During the tournament, the U.S. team (consisting entirely of major league players) failed to reach the semifinal round. The two semifinal games pitted Japan against South Korea and Cuba against the Dominican Republic. In the championship game, the Japanese team prevailed over Cuba. Japan also won the second World Baseball Classic in 2009.

and Venezuela. Their seasons are played between October and January. The winners of the four leagues then meet in the Caribbean Series each February. Mexico, Venezuela, and the Dominican Republic also have summer leagues that are affiliated with the minor leagues in the United States.

ASIA

Japan was the first Asian country to take up baseball. The game was introduced there in the 1870s. It quickly gained a national following. Japan's first professional league was created in 1936. The current Central and Pacific leagues began play in 1950. Every October the two league champions compete in the Japan Series, Japanese baseball's version of the World Series.

In 1995 pitcher Hideo Nomo became the first Japanese citizen to play in the North American major leagues. At that time many major league fans were skeptical that a Japanese player could succeed in North America. Nomo had an impressive season in 1995, earning the National League's rookie of the year award and proving the quality of Japanese baseball. Many of Nomo's countrymen soon followed him to the major leagues.

The most notable of these players was outfielder Ichiro Suzuki. In 2004 Suzuki's 262 hits surpassed George Sisler's long-standing record for the most hits in a single season.

Baseball is also an important sport in South Korea and Taiwan. The Korea Baseball Organization started a professional league that played its first game in 1982. Taiwan's Chinese Professional Baseball League first began play in 1990. Additionally, Taiwan is well known for the championship-winning Little League teams it has produced.

On the mound for the Los Angeles Dodgers, Hideo Nomo makes his major league debut on May 2, 1995. **Otto Greule Jr./Getty Images**

CHAPTER 2
PLAYING THE GAME

The two teams in a baseball game alternate positions as batters (offense) and fielders (defense). They exchange places when three members of the batting team are "put out" by the fielding team. As batters, players try to hit the ball out of the reach of the fielders and make a complete circuit around the bases for a run. After nine innings, the team with the most runs wins the game.

THE FIELD AND EQUIPMENT

A baseball field is divided into the infield and the outfield. Ordinarily, the infield has a dirt surface, and the outfield is covered with grass. Within the infield is a square area called the diamond, which has four white bases, one on each corner. One of the bases is a five-sided rubber slab called home plate.

Official Baseball Playing Field

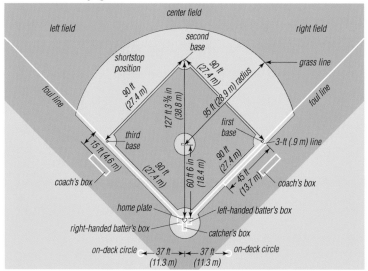

Additional Dimensions
1st, 2nd, and 3rd bases–15 in x 15 in
(38.1 cm x 38.1 cm)
Home plate–17 in x 17 in (43.2 cm x 43.2 cm)
Distance from home plate to batters' boxes–6 in
(15.2 cm)
Batters' boxes–4 ft x 6 ft (1.2 m x 1.8 m)
Pitcher's plate–24 in x 6 in (61 cm x 15.2 cm)
Catcher's box–3 ft 7 in wide x 8 ft long
(1.1 m wide x 2.4 m long)
On-deck circles–5 ft diameter (1.5 m diameter)
Coaches' boxes–20 ft wide x 10 ft deep
(6.1 m wide x 3 m deep)

In this diagram of an official baseball playing field, the beige surfaces within the field are bare ground. The remaining surface is grass or artificial turf. Home plate is five-sided; bases are square. **Encyclopædia Britannica, Inc.**

On the standard baseball field the bases are 90 feet (27.4 meters) apart. In the center of the diamond is the pitcher's mound, a small dirt mound located 60 feet 6 inches (18.4 meters) from home plate.

BALL AND BATS

The ball must be between 9 and 9¼ inches (23 to 23.5 centimeters) in circumference and

must weigh not less than 5 or more than 5¼ ounces (142 and 149 grams). The rules require that it have a small core of cork, rubber, or similar material wound over with yarn and covered with two strips of white leather stitched together.

Bats are limited to a maximum of 2¾ inches (7 centimeters) in diameter and 42 inches (107 centimeters) in length, but may be of any weight. The bat should be made

An official regulation baseball. Shutterstock.com

from a single piece of wood or laminated wood with its grain parallel to the length of the bat. Aluminum bats are not permitted in professional play.

Baseball bats at the ready in a dugout. **Driendl Group/Photodisc/ Getty Images**

GLOVES

The typical baseball glove is made of leather held together with stitching and filled with some padding. The catcher wears a heavily padded mitt that is no more than 38 inches (96.5 centimeters) in circumference and no more than 15½ inches (39.4 centimeters) from top to bottom. All of the other players wear long-fingered gloves that cannot exceed a length of 12 inches (30.5 centimeters). Leather lacing connects the fingertips of the glove to each other. Leather webbing fills the space between the thumb and index finger. The first baseman's mitt is usually thinner and more flexible than the other players' gloves.

OFFENSE

The visiting team gets to bat first. The team's manager (head coach) decides in advance the order in which the players will bat, and they (or their substitutes) must follow that order throughout the game. This batting order is known as the lineup. Usually the best hitters bat toward the beginning of the lineup.

Fans often bring their own gloves to professional ball games in hopes of catching a ball. **Donald Miralle/Getty Images**

29

Hits and Runs

A run is scored every time a player has made a complete circuit of the bases and returned to home plate. To get on base the batter tries to hit the pitched ball anywhere in fair territory, yet beyond the reach of a fielder trying to catch the ball before it touches the ground. The batter (now called the runner) must then reach at least first base before the ball is recovered and thrown or carried to the base ahead of him. A ball batted safely in this way is counted as a hit.

Types of Hits

A ball hit far enough to permit the batter to reach first base safely is called a single. A hit good for two bases is called a double, and one good for three bases is called a triple. When a ball is hit out of the playing field in fair territory, or if fielders cannot throw the runner out before he reaches home plate, the hit is good for four bases—a home run. If the first batter singles and the second batter does likewise, the first batter is advanced to second or third base. Then if the third batter should hit a home run, his teammates on base will score ahead of him for a total of

Endy Chávez of the New York Mets makes it safely, if somewhat awk-wardly, to first base, past Albert Pujols of the St. Louis Cardinals, in a 2008 game. **New York Daily News Archive/Getty Images**

three runs. A home run hit when the bases are loaded—that is, when there are runners on first, second, and third base—scores four runs and is called a grand slam.

DEFENSE

The aim of the defensive team in the field is to keep the batters from scoring runs. To do so, the fielders try to record three outs before an opponent can reach home plate. When three offensive players have been declared out, the batting team is retired. The defense records outs by striking out the batter, catching a ball on the fly, throwing the batter out, or tagging out a base runner.

BALLS AND STRIKES

The defensive team's pitcher throws the ball to each batter on the opposing team. The pitcher can record one type of out by throwing three strikes to the batter. A strike is counted when the batter swings at the pitched ball and misses or fails to swing at a pitched ball that passes through the strike zone. (The strike zone is an imaginary rectangular area above home plate. An umpire standing behind home plate judges which pitched balls are strikes.) A ball knocked into foul territory is a strike except when a batter already has two strikes against him, in which case the foul ball does not count for anything. A foul tip (a ball glancing slightly

Home plate umpire Todd Tichenor calls strike three at a 2009 game between the Pittsburgh Pirates and the Arizona Diamondbacks. Christian Petersen/Getty Images

off the bat) counts as a strike when caught by the catcher.

If the pitcher fails to throw the ball through the strike zone and the batter lets it go by, the umpire calls the pitch a "ball." If the pitcher throws four balls to any one batter, the batter advances to first base. The four balls constitute a walk; that is, the batter gets to go to first base without having to hit and run. The batter also gets to advance to first base if a pitched ball hits any part of his body—as long as an effort was made to dodge the pitch.

FIELDING

The real work of the other players in the field begins when the batter hits a fair ball. If it is a fly ball or a line drive, the fielders try to catch it before it falls to the ground. A batted ball that is caught in the air (in either fair or foul territory) counts as an out. If the batted ball is a grounder to the infield, the fielders try to scoop it up and throw it to first base ahead of the runner for an out.

Another type of out is recorded when a fielder with the ball tags (touches with the ball) the base runner while he is off the base. This sometimes occurs when the runner

Infielder Jayson Nix of the Colorado Rockies tries to tag Scott Podsenik of the Chicago White Sox during a spring training game in 2005. **Brian Bahr/Getty Images**

attempts to advance by stealing a base. During a force play, a runner may be forced out by a fielder who throws the ball to the base ahead. For example, a base runner on first base is forced to run to second when the batter hits a ground ball and runs to first base. If the ball reaches second base before the runner does, the runner is out.

An out also can be recorded against an advancing base runner if a fielder catches a batted ball before it touches the ground. The batter who hit the ball is out—and the rules require the base runner to return to base before a fielder with the ball tags him or the base. If there are other runners trying to advance from other bases, the defensive team usually tries to put out the player nearest home plate. This defensive tactic retires the base runner most likely to score a run.

THE PITCHER

The most important defensive player is the pitcher. He has the job of making the opposing batter miss the ball or else hit it where it

Tom Seaver displays classic pitching form as he throws for the New York Mets during a game in the mid-1960s. **Louis Requena/MLB Photos via Getty Images**

can be fielded by teammates. A good pitcher may use several kinds of pitches, such as a fastball, a slider, a split-fingered fastball, a curveball, a change-up, or a knuckleball. By using a variety of pitches, the pitcher can keep the batter guessing as to which type

of pitch is coming. Above all, a pitcher must have control—the ability to throw the ball where he aims it.

In most cases, a pitcher's primary weapon is the fastball. Its sheer speed makes it difficult to hit. Good fastball pitchers are capable of throwing the ball 100 miles (160 kilometers) per hour. Another fast pitch is the slider. Almost as fast as a fastball, it also curves, or breaks, sideways slightly. A third type of speed pitch, the split-fingered fastball, deceives the batter because it drops sharply downward as it reaches home plate.

A pitch called a change-up is used to fool a batter expecting a fastball. It is delivered with a pitching motion that imitates the delivery of a fastball, but it is thrown at a much slower speed. A curveball is slower in speed than a fastball, but the break in a good curveball may be as great as a foot or more. The trick to throwing a curveball lies in the spinning motion given the ball as it leaves the pitcher's hand. If a right-handed pitcher throws a curveball that breaks away from a right-handed batter, it is considered a traditional curve; if it breaks toward the batter, it is sometimes called a screwball. The knuckleball is a seldom-used pitch, but its irregular, wobbling ball flight makes it extremely difficult to hit.

THE INFIELDERS

The other infield positions include the first baseman, the second baseman, the short-stop, the third baseman, and the catcher. Aside from the pitcher, the catcher is the most important player on the defensive team. The catcher stands or crouches behind home plate clad in a mask, chest protector, shin guards, and a heavily padded glove. He catches all pitches that go by the batter and guards home plate when an advancing runner attempts to score. A good catcher knows an opposing batter's weaknesses and sends secret hand signals to the pitcher regarding the type of pitch to throw.

It is the duty of the remaining infielders to prevent batted balls from going into the out-field for base hits. They are also responsible for tagging out or forcing out runners. The first and third basemen guard the areas around their bases. The shortstop and second base-man occupy positions to the left and right, respectively, of second base. They must work in tandem to cover that base and the middle of the infield.

The coordinated efforts of the infielders can prevent many runs from being scored. One of the most exciting defensive feats in

Johnny Bench, seen here in the 1970s, established himself as one of the game's finest catchers during his 17 seasons with the Cincinnati Reds. He won 10 consecutive Gold Glove awards (1968–77) and had an exceptional throwing arm. **Focus On Sport/Getty Images**

baseball is the double play, which records two outs during one at bat. The most common double play occurs when a runner is on first base, and a ground ball is hit to the shortstop. The shortstop fields the ball and quickly throws it to second base ahead of the advancing runner. The second baseman catches the shortstop's throw, touches second base for the force-out, and then pivots and throws the ball to the first baseman to retire the batter running to first.

THE OUTFIELDERS

The outfielders go after long fly balls or the ground balls that are batted past the infield. Outfielders must be good judges of ball flight in order to chase and catch long hits. The best are also strong and accurate throwers capable of rifling the ball back into the infield, in some cases as far as home plate. As batters, outfielders are usually a team's best hitters.

THE UMPIRES

All baseball games must have at least one umpire to call balls and strikes and to rule on the various plays. Major league games usually have four umpires, one at each base. World Series games use six umpires, with the two extra officials stationed along each foul line.

LENGTH OF A GAME

Nine innings make a normal game unless the home team is ahead at the end of 8½ innings. In that case, the game is complete. If the score is tied at the end of the ninth inning, the teams play additional innings until one side wins or until the game is called because of darkness or for some other reason.

41

The grounds crew at Boston's Fenway Park haul a field-covering tarp behind them as rain delays a game in the spring of 2010. Elsa/Getty Images

Sometimes play is halted by rain, darkness, or some other cause before nine innings are completed. If five (four and one half, if the home team is ahead) or more innings have been played, the game is counted as official. If less than this amount has been played, the game is canceled.

CHAPTER 3

HISTORY OF THE GAME

In 1907 American entrepreneur A.G. Spalding created a commission to discover the origin of baseball. The commission was eager to promote the distinctive American sport and disprove theories that the game derived from English stick-and-ball games such as rounders and cricket. The commission concluded that a man named Abner Doubleday created the rules of baseball in 1839 in Cooperstown, N.Y. Subsequent historical research, however, discredited this story. Baseball did indeed evolve from games such as rounders, which was a popular recreation in North America as far back as the late 1700s. The first set of baseball rules was established in 1845 by the New York Knickerbocker Base Ball Club, an organization of amateur players led by Alexander J. Cartwright. The rules were much like those for rounders but with some significant differences. Many of the 1845 rules still remain.

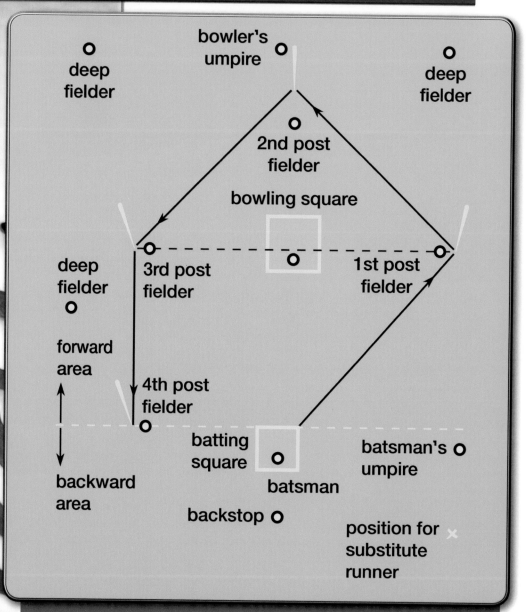

Rounders field with player positions. An old English game that never became a seriously competitive sport, rounders is probably an ancestor of baseball. **Encyclopædia Britannica, Inc.**

EARLY YEARS

Early baseball clubs were strictly amateur, but after the American Civil War (1861–65), commercial interests began to take over the sport. The first all-professional team, the Cincinnati Red Stockings, was formed in 1869; the first professional league was formed in 1871. The National League of Professional Baseball Clubs (now simply known as the National League) was founded in 1876 with eight teams. The American League began as the Western League in 1893. It consisted largely of clubs from Midwestern cities. The first World Series was held in 1903.

The major leagues matured quickly, and by the turn of the 20th century the professional game was a national obsession. Managers Connie Mack of the Philadelphia Athletics and John McGraw of the New York Giants emerged as the great tacticians of the game. They are credited for creating the style of play known as inside baseball, a style that featured speedy players who could steal bases and skillful batters who could bunt and slap base hits all over the field.

The sport experienced a major setback in 1920 when it was discovered that members of the Chicago White Sox had accepted bribes

The first nine players of the Cincinnati Red Stockings, 1869. Buyenlarge/
Archive Photos/Getty Images

from gamblers to throw games in the 1919 World Series. What became known as the Black Sox Scandal led to the creation of the office of the commissioner of baseball. The commissioner was charged with protecting the integrity and best interests of the sport. Kenesaw Landis, the first commissioner, was

York Times.

WEDNESDAY, SEPTEMBER 29, 1920. TWO CENTS

EIGHT WHITE SOX PLAYERS ARE INDICTED ON CHARGE OF FIXING 1919 WORLD SERIES; CICOTTE GOT $10,000 AND JACKSON $5,000

Yankee Owners Give Praise to Comiskey And Offer Him Use of Their Whole Team

COMISKEY SUSPENDS THEM

Following the announcement from Chicago yesterday that Owner Charles A. Comiskey had suspended two star pitchers, two regular infielders, his two leading outfielders and one utility player, Colonels Jacob Ruppert and T. L. Huston, owners of the New York Club, put

Promises to Run Them Out of Baseball if

Front page headline of the **New York Times** *reporting on the Black Sox Scandal, Sept. 29, 1920.* **New York Times Co./Archive Photos/ Getty Images**

ORIGIN OF THE WORLD SERIES

The supremacy of the National League was challenged by several rival organizations in its early years. Of these rivals, only the American League survived. Founded as the Western League in 1893, it changed its name to the American League of Professional Baseball Clubs after the 1899 season and declared itself a major league in 1901. As the American League moved teams into new cities, the National League objected.

During the subsequent "baseball war," the American League wooed away many of the National League's star players. In 1903 the leagues agreed to prohibit single ownership of two clubs in the same city and the shifting of franchises from one city to another by either league without permission of the other. They also established rules for transferring players from one league to the other and for moving minor league players into the major leagues. The peace of 1903 resulted in the first World Series, in which Boston, of the American League, defeated Pittsburgh, of the National League.

appointed in 1920 and issued a lifetime ban from baseball for the eight Chicago players involved in the scandal.

In the 1920s and '30s major league baseball enjoyed a golden era that starred New York Yankees outfielder Babe Ruth. A large man with an even larger personality, Ruth possessed a sense of fun and confidence that seemed to capture the mood of the country during the 1920s. Ruth's prowess for hitting home runs also revolutionized the sport, bringing an end to the era of inside baseball.

ISSUES OF RACE

Before baseball clubs were formally organized into leagues, games between black and white clubs frequently occurred in Northern cities. Racially mixed teams also existed. But in 1867 the first formal organization of baseball clubs, the National Association of Base Ball Players, issued a rule stating that clubs "which may be composed of one or more colored persons" should not be permitted to compete with its teams of white amateurs. When the first professional league was formed four years later, it had no written rule barring black players, but it was tacitly understood that they were not welcome.

NEGRO LEAGUES

Professional African American ballplayers turned to the practice of barnstorming to make a living. Barnstorming involved traveling across the country looking for teams and games

Rube Foster, often called the "Father of Black Baseball," pictured in 1909. **Chicago History Museum/Archive Photos/Getty Images**

to play. They also sought out professional opportunities in the Caribbean and Mexican leagues. Several attempts were made to organize black professional leagues, and they met with varying success. The first league to really succeed was the Negro National League. Rube Foster, a talented pitcher and owner of the Chicago American Giants, founded the league in 1920. Foster's National League lasted until 1931. That league plus several others that thrived through the 1930s and '40s are known collectively as the Negro Leagues.

Teams such as the Homestead (Pennsylvania) Grays and the Kansas City Monarchs gained national reputations for their excellent play. On occasions the Negro League teams would play exhibition games against major league teams, and they often won. All-time greats such as Josh Gibson, James "Cool Papa" Bell, and Buck Leonard played their entire careers outside of major league baseball. The Negro Leagues also served as a haven for Latin American ballplayers who were dark-skinned.

BLACKS IN THE MAJOR LEAGUES

The unwritten rule barring black ballplayers from competing alongside white players

Brooklyn Dodgers' manager Leo Durocher shakes hands with Jackie Robinson in March 1947. **New York Daily News Archive/Getty Images**

continued until 1947, when Jackie Robinson debuted for the Brooklyn Dodgers of the National League. Robinson endured racial taunts and hostility from fans and players in order to prove that blacks belonged in the major leagues. Later that same year, Larry Doby signed with the Cleveland Indians, thus integrating the American League. In the years that followed, more and more black players claimed roster spots in the major leagues. The acceptance of black ballplayers in the major leagues led to a talent shortage in the Negro Leagues. By the 1960s the Negro Leagues had disappeared.

MOVEMENT AND EXPANSION

Integration was not the only major change faced by the major leagues after World War II. Despite an excellent product on the field, teams experienced declining attendance. Many families had moved to the suburbs and found the decaying old ballparks uncomfortable and difficult to reach by automobile. Meanwhile, cities in the southern and western United States were growing rapidly. These emerging cities were eager to lure major league clubs with their large fan base and new stadiums.

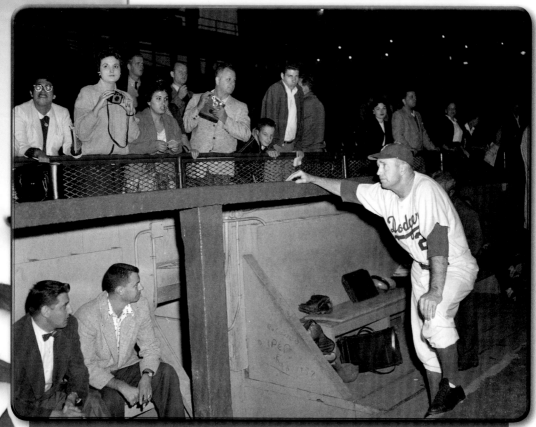

This photograph, taken on Sept. 24, 1957, shows a wistful-looking Walter "Smokey" Alston, manager of the Brooklyn Dodgers, at the team's last game at Ebbets Field. The field was demolished in 1960. **Rogers Photo Archive/Getty Images**

The 1950s saw the first team relocations in more than half a century. In 1953 the Braves left Boston for Milwaukee (in 1966, the Braves moved again, to Atlanta). Several other teams also moved in the next few years. None of those moves, however, had the impact of the decision by the owners of the Brooklyn Dodgers and New York Giants to move to California in 1958. Devoted New Yorkers felt deeply betrayed when these two longtime baseball rivals abandoned their region. The newly minted Los Angeles Dodgers and San Francisco Giants, however, thrived in their new stadiums.

This period of franchise movement was followed by a long period of expansion. Between 1961 and 1977 the number of major league teams expanded from 16 teams (eight in each league) to 26 teams (14 in the American League and 12 in the National League). This included adding two clubs in the Canadian cities of Montreal and Toronto.

CHAPTER 4
THE MODERN GAME

As the major leagues grew in the 1960s and '70s, they also introduced important structural changes to increase revenue and maintain fan interest. Early in the 1960s both the American and the National leagues expanded the traditional 154-game season to 162 games. In 1969 each league was split into two divisions, and a round of divisional play-offs was added to the postseason. On the field, the American League's 1973 introduction of the designated-hitter rule was intended to increase the number of hits during a game. This innovative rule allowed skilled batsmen to hit in place of traditionally weak-hitting pitchers. More recent decades have seen more expansion, innovations, and record-setting performances as well as controversy, with well-publicized labor issues and a steroid scandal tarnishing the reputation of the game.

FURTHER EXPANSION AND INNOVATIONS

Another round of expansion beginning in the 1990s grew the league to its current 30 teams and three-division league structure. The American League added the Tampa Bay Devil Rays. The National League added the Arizona Diamondbacks, Colorado Rockies, Florida Marlins, and Washington (D.C.) Nationals.

Innovations occurred during the expansion period as well. In addition to the new divisional structure, in 1995 the first wild-card teams appeared in the play-offs. This gave a fourth team in each league a chance to win the World Series. Another innovation came in 1997 when interleague play was introduced, allowing American and National league teams to play each other during the regular season. Fans could now see their local team play clubs from the other league. This also helped answer one of baseball's long-standing arguments—which league had the better teams. Interleague play heightened fan interest even more in cities with crosstown rivals in different leagues, such as Chicago, Los Angeles, and New York.

LABOR ISSUES

The latter part of the 20th century saw a dramatic increase in the amount of money that players earned. The average salary of a baseball player rose from around $41,000 in 1974 to nearly $2,000,000 in 2000. The reason for this increase was the advent of free agency in 1977.

Catcher Brian Schneider of the New York Mets tags out Johnny Damon of the New York Yankees in the 2008 "subway series." **Jim McIsaac/ Getty Images**

FREE AGENCY

Since the early days of the major leagues, players were prohibited from selling their services to a different club because of baseball's Reserve Clause. This agreement, dating from 1879, ensured the rights of each team to the services of its players. This meant that a team could prevent its players from seeking better pay from other teams.

In the 1960s the Major League Baseball Players Association (a players' union founded in 1953) began a campaign to remove the Reserve Clause. After several important court cases and a 13-day midseason strike in 1972, the union finally forced the owners to accept free agency. As free agents in the baseball market, players not under contract could sell their services to any team they liked. With team owners now bidding competitively for players, salaries quickly began to rise.

STRIKES

The rules for free agency and the growth of salaries have remained an issue between owners and the players' union. Disagreements between the two led to strikes in 1981 (50 days) and 1985 (two days). In both instances,

the owners agreed to player demands, largely because the teams were still profitable due to network television revenues.

In the early 1990s, however, television money became scarcer, yet players' salaries continued to increase. In 1994 owners proposed new rules on free agency and a salary cap. (A salary cap is a predetermined limit on how much a team can spend on payroll.) The union rejected the proposal and went on strike. The 1994–95 strike lasted 234 days, spread across two baseball seasons, and forced the cancellation of the 1994 World Series — the first time a World Series had been canceled since 1904. The players announced that the strike was over after a federal judge forced the owners to operate under the old contract. The owners accepted the players' offer to return without a new agreement and to continue negotiations. Thus the strike ended without a true resolution.

RENEWED INTEREST

Professional baseball alienated many fans when the 1994 World Series was canceled. In subsequent years, however, several exciting seasons helped to rekindle interest in the game. In 1998 the long-standing

SPORTSMEN OF THE YEAR
MARK McGWIRE *and* SAMMY SOSA

This 1998 Sports Illustrated cover features Sportsmen of the Year Mark McGwire of the St. Louis Cardinals and Sammy Sosa of the Chicago Cubs. Walter Iooss Jr./Sports Illustrated/Getty Images

single-season home run record was broken during a thrilling power-hitting exhibition by two players, Mark McGwire of the St. Louis Cardinals and Sammy Sosa of the Chicago Cubs. By season's end, both players had surpassed the old record of 61 home runs (set by Roger Maris in 1961), with McGwire tallying 70 home runs and Sosa 66. Incredibly, the new mark established by McGwire was

Jubilant Chicago White Sox players celebrate after winning the 2005 World Series against the Houston Astros, 4 games to 0. Lisa Blumenfeld/Getty Images

broken again just a few seasons later, when Barry Bonds of the San Francisco Giants hit 73 home runs in 2001. In 2007 Bonds hit his 756th career home run to break one of the most hallowed records in sports, Hank Aaron's mark of 755 lifetime home runs.

The World Series also provided drama. The New York Yankees won three World Series in a row, from 1998 to 2000. Perhaps even more exciting were the back-to-back championships of two teams that had not been World Series winners since the 1910s. In 2004 the Boston Red Sox won their first World Series since 1918, and in 2005 the Chicago White Sox became World Series champions for the first time since 1917.

THE STEROID SCANDAL

The proliferation of home runs in the 1990s helped to revive the game, but it also gave rise to a scandal. Rumors began to circulate about the use of performance-enhancing drugs by ballplayers. Some of baseball's best hitters were suspected of taking steroids, and a few former players confessed to having used them. Barry Bonds testified before a grand jury that he had never knowingly taken steroids. Accusations of steroid use dogged his

Barry Bonds. Robert Laberge/Getty Images

pursuit of Aaron's career home run record, however, and in 2007 he was indicted for perjury and obstruction of justice regarding his testimony. Other prominent players whose accomplishments were called into question by the steroid issue included Mark McGwire and Sammy Sosa. In 2005 they were among a group of players who testified before a congressional panel in Washington about steroid use in the major leagues; the baseball commissioner and the director of the players' union also took part. As a result of the hearing, the penalties for steroid use were strengthened. The toughest of the new penalties against an offending player was a lifetime suspension from baseball.

The scandal still did not fade away, however. In 2006 Major League Baseball Commissioner Bud Selig named former U.S. senator George Mitchell to lead an independent investigation into steroid use in baseball. Mitchell's report, released in 2007, named 86 current and former players—including such stars as Bonds, Roger Clemens, Miguel Tejada, and Andy Pettitte—who were alleged to have possessed or used either steroids or human growth hormone (HGH) in the previous decade. Mitchell noted that everyone in baseball—players and management alike— shared responsibility for the "steroids era" and the effect it had on baseball's reputation with the public.

CHAPTER 5

NOTABLE PLAYERS

I n its long history, baseball has seen a great number of outstanding players. Some are known for their hitting, some for their pitching or fielding, and some for their all-around skills. Some players are also distinguished for reasons that transcend the game, such as Jackie Robinson and his role in the civil rights movement. This chapter introduces just a few of these notable players, including several legends as well as contemporary players who will no doubt join them in the Hall of Fame someday.

HALL OF FAMERS

BABE RUTH

The crowd that jammed Chicago's Wrigley Field booed when the big man with the barrel-shaped body and pipestem legs came up to bat. It was the third game of the 1932 World Series between the Chicago Cubs and the New York Yankees. The score was 4–4 in the fifth inning. Cub pitcher Charlie Root threw one strike, then another. Grinning, the batter stepped back and seemed to point to the distant center-field bleachers. Root pitched, the big man swung, and the ball soared into the bleachers for a home run. The hitter was Babe Ruth, probably the most revered of baseball players. Ruth's legendary pointing gesture—whether it ever happened or whether he even intended it—captured the imagination of baseball fans, as did everything about this great player.

Babe Ruth. **UPI**

The Babe's achievements loom large in the record books. The left-hander held or shared about 60 records, with 28 made in World Series games. Among them were his record of pitching 29 consecutive scoreless innings in World Series play and his total of 714 major league homers—not including 15 World Series homers. (The pitching

and home run records were later broken by Whitey Ford and Hank Aaron.)

George Herman Ruth was born in Baltimore, Md., on Feb. 6, 1895. In 1914 he began to play baseball with the Baltimore Orioles of the International League. The Orioles' manager, Jack Dunn, paid him $600 for his first season. Although Ruth later earned such nicknames as the Sultan of Swat and the Busting Bambino, he got his most famous nickname—Babe—on his first day of practice. A veteran coach sneered at the 6-foot-2 youngster, "Here's another one of Dunn's babes."

Later in the season, he was sold to the Boston Red Sox. As his batting prowess grew, he was shifted from the pitcher's mound to the outfield, where he could play every day. Before he quit pitching, Ruth had won 94 games and lost 46.

In 1920 Ruth was sold for $125,000 to the New York Yankees, whose stadium was later called the House That Ruth Built. Then began the greatest years of his career. He reached his peak in 1927, when he hit 60 home runs, a season record (for 154 games) that still stands. As Ruth grew older, his huge body became too heavy for his slender legs. In 1935, after 15 years with the Yankees, he joined the Boston

Braves as a playing vice president. Before the season ended, the unhappy Ruth laid down his bat for the last time. He ended his career in baseball as a coach for the Brooklyn Dodgers in 1938. Ruth died in New York City on Aug. 16, 1948.

JACKIE ROBINSON

"A life is not important except in the impact it has on other lives," reads the tombstone of Jackie Robinson, the first African American athlete to play in baseball's major leagues in the 20th century. By breaking the color barrier in 1947, Robinson made great strides not only for black athletes but also for all concerned with racial justice.

Jack Roosevelt Robinson was born on Jan. 31, 1919, in Cairo, Ga., but grew up in Pasadena, Calif. He excelled at baseball, football, basketball, and track at the University of California at Los Angeles (UCLA). He left UCLA in 1941 and briefly played professional football before being drafted into the U.S. Army. During his service, he refused to sit at the back of a bus and was threatened with a court-martial, but the charges were dropped and he was given an honorable discharge in 1945.

Jackie Robinson, 1946. **UPI**

While playing baseball for the Kansas City Monarchs in the Negro National League, Robinson caught the eye of a scout for the Brooklyn (now Los Angeles) Dodgers and was brought to the attention of team president Branch Rickey. Major league baseball was closed to black players at the time. Rickey thought that this was wrong, and he wanted to find someone who could successfully integrate the sport. After meeting Robinson and being impressed with his courage as well as his skill, Rickey signed him to a Dodger minor league team.

Robinson made his major league debut in 1947. The chief problem he had to overcome was controlling his fiery temper in the face of continual racial slurs from the crowds and other ballplayers, including some of his own teammates. Robinson did not break his promise to Rickey to remain silent, though pitchers sometimes deliberately threw at him, hotels at away games often would not accommodate him, and he and his family received death threats. He instead let his actions do the talking by batting .297 and leading the National League (NL) in stolen bases. He was chosen rookie of the year at season's end.

Robinson's .342 average made him the league's batting champion and Most Valuable Player (MVP) in 1949. During his career, which he spent primarily as a second baseman, Robinson helped the Dodgers capture six NL pennants and one World Series title. He retired in 1956 with a .311 lifetime batting average and 197 total stolen bases. When he was elected to the Baseball Hall of Fame in 1962, he was the first black player to be so honored. Robinson died in Stamford, Conn., on Oct. 24, 1972.

HANK AARON

"Throwing a fastball by Henry Aaron is like trying to sneak sunrise past a rooster," St. Louis pitcher Curt Simmons once said, expressing the frustration that pitchers around the league felt while facing one of the most prolific power hitters in major league baseball history. By the start of the 1974 season, Aaron had already rewritten the sport's record book with his stellar and remarkably

consistent batting statistics. The most storied moment of his career, however, was yet to come. On April 8, Hammerin' Hank electrified Atlanta-Fulton County Stadium—and the country—by surpassing the legendary Babe Ruth with his 715th home run, shattering a record that many experts had long considered untouchable.

Henry Louis Aaron was born on Feb. 5, 1934, in Mobile, Ala. At age 16, he began playing shortstop with the semiprofessional Mobile Black Bears. The next year Aaron was signed by the Indianapolis Clowns of the Negro American League. He spent just a few months with the Clowns in 1952 before his contract was bought by the Boston Braves, who assigned him to the minor leagues. Aaron joined the Braves, who had moved to Milwaukee, as an outfielder in 1954. In 1956 he won the first of his two National League batting titles with an average of .328. Aaron was named the NL Most Valuable Player in 1957 after his .322 average and league-leading

Hank Aaron, 1974. Herb Scharfman/Sports Imagery/Getty Images

44 home runs and 132 runs batted in (RBI) helped the Braves capture their first World Series title.

By the time the Braves moved to Atlanta at the end of 1965, Aaron had hit 398 home runs. A few years later, his pursuit of baseball's most celebrated record—Ruth's all-time home run mark—was accompanied by both an intense media blitz and a display of racial intolerance. In 1972 Aaron started receiving hate mail, including death threats, from some baseball fans who were upset to find an African American on the verge of overtaking one of the country's most beloved sports heroes. Aaron quietly withstood the pressure with his characteristic cool, but after breaking the record he began using his standing to speak out against the injustices of baseball. Aaron retired after the 1976 season with more career records than any other player in major league history up to that time, including totals of 755 home runs, 2,297 RBI, and 1,477 extra-base hits. He was voted into the Baseball Hall of Fame in 1982.

WILLIE MAYS

Willie Mays was an outstanding baseball player known for both his batting and his

fielding. He ranks among the all-time leaders in home runs, hits, runs scored, and runs batted in. He was also known for his spectacular leaping and diving catches. Many consider him to have been the best all-around player in the history of the game.

Willie Howard Mays was born in Westfield, Ala., on May 6, 1931. In 1948, while he was still in high school, he joined the Birmingham Black Barons of the Negro National League. The New York Giants of the National League bought his contract when he graduated from high school in 1950. After two seasons in the minor leagues, Mays went to the Giants in 1951 and was named rookie of the year at the end of that season.

After serving in the U.S. Army for two years, Mays returned to baseball for the 1954 season. He led the league in hitting (.345) and had 41 home runs, helping the Giants win the NL pennant and the World Series, In 1966 his two-year contract with the Giants (who had moved to San Francisco in 1958) gave him the highest salary of any baseball player of that time. He was traded to the New York Mets midseason in 1972 and retired after the 1973 season. Late in his career, he played in the infield, mainly at first base. Mays retired with 660 home

Willie Mays. **Robert Riger/Getty Images**

runs, 3,283 hits, 2,062 runs scored, and 1,903 RBI. He led the league in home runs in 1955, 1962, and 1964–65, won 12 consecutive Gold Gloves (1957–68), and appeared in 24 All-Star Games. He was elected to the Baseball Hall of Fame in 1979.

CONTEMPORARY PLAYERS

RANDY JOHNSON

With a blistering fastball and an imposing 6-foot 10-inch (2-meter) frame, Randy Johnson quickly built a reputation as the pitcher major leaguers most feared facing. He won five career Cy Young Awards as the best pitcher in either the American or National League.

Randall David Johnson was born on Sept. 10, 1963, in Walnut Creek, Calif. He earned a scholarship to the University of Southern California, where he played basketball for a few years and starred on the baseball team from 1983 to 1985. He made his major league debut in 1988 with the National League Montreal Expos.

Johnson was named to the first of his 10 All-Star Games in 1990 as a member of the American League Seattle Mariners. Johnson led the AL in strikeouts for four consecutive years (1992–95), and in 1995 he won the AL Cy Young Award.

After the 1998 season, Johnson signed with the NL Arizona Diamondbacks. He led the NL in earned run average, innings pitched, and strikeouts on his way to the 1999 NL Cy Young Award. Johnson won Cy Youngs in each of the following three seasons. His

Randy Johnson, 2009. **Otto Greule Jr./Getty Images**

most impressive feat, however, took place at the 2001 World Series, where he tied a record with three wins in a single World Series while guiding the Diamondbacks to their first championship.

After pitching for two seasons with the New York Yankees, Johnson was traded in 2007 to Arizona for a second stint with the Diamondbacks. The following year, he recorded his 4,673rd strikeout, passing Roger Clemens for second place on the all-time strikeouts list—behind only Nolan Ryan. Johnson signed with the San Francisco Giants after the 2008 season. In 2009 he recorded the 300th victory of his career, a landmark that had been reached by only 23 other big-league pitchers. Johnson retired in 2010.

DEREK JETER

The New York Yankees won the World Series in 1998, 1999, and 2000, becoming the first team to win three consecutive champion-ships since 1974. Key to the team's dominance was shortstop Derek Jeter, a hugely popu-lar player and a perennial member of the American League All-Star team.

Derek Sanderson Jeter was born in Pequannock, N.J., on June 26, 1974. After an

Derek Jeter. **New York Daily News Archive/Getty Images**

impressive high school baseball record, he was drafted by the Yankees as a first-round pick in 1992. He spent a few years improving his skills in the minor leagues before becoming the starting shortstop for the Yankees in 1996.

In his first season, Jeter posted a batting average of .314 and had 78 RBI. He was named AL rookie of the year, and the Yankees won the World Series. Jeter continued to play a vital role in the Yankees' success as the team won the World Series in 1998, 1999, 2000, and 2009. With his consistent and timely hitting, Jeter acquired a reputation as one of the premier postseason hitters in baseball. In 2000 he was named MVP of the All-Star Game and the World Series.

From 2004 to 2006 Jeter won three consecutive AL Gold Glove awards as the best-fielding shortstop in the league. In 2009 he recorded his 2,674th career hit, breaking the record for the most hits by a shortstop in major league history.

ALBERT PUJOLS

First baseman Albert Pujols ranks among a select group of baseball players who hit consistently for both average and power. Even early in his career, he was already considered to be one of the game's greatest hitters.

José Alberto Pujols Alcántara was born on Jan. 16, 1980, in Santo Domingo, the capital of the Dominican Republic. The Pujols family immigrated to the United States when Albert was 16, and they eventually settled in Missouri. Pujols impressed major league scouts with his play at both the high school and collegiate level, and he was selected by the St. Louis Cardinals in the 1999 draft. In 2001, he earned a spot on the Cardinals' roster.

Presumed to be a reserve as he entered his first season, Pujols instead played his way into the starting lineup. He posted a .329 batting average with 37 home runs and 130 runs batted in (RBI), and he was the unanimous choice for 2001 National League rookie of the year. Pujols continued to put up impressive offensive numbers in the following seasons and collected a number of awards, including the 2004 NL Championship Series MVP and Silver Slugger awards in 2001, 2003, and 2004. In 2005 he hit .330 with 41 home runs and 117 RBI and was named NL MVP.

Albert Pujols, 2010. **Kevin C. Cox/Getty Images**

In 2006 Pujols bettered the batting statistics of his previous season, hitting .331 with 49 home runs and 137 RBI. That year he also helped lead St. Louis to a World Series title. In 2008 Pujols was named NL MVP after finishing the season with a .357 batting average and 116 RBI. The following year he won his third NL MVP award after hitting .327 with 47 home runs and 135 RBI.

ICHIRO SUZUKI

Ichiro Suzuki was widely recognized as the best baseball player in Japan before coming to the United States. Because pitchers in the American major leagues throw harder than their Japanese counterparts, some observers believed that Suzuki would struggle at the plate. He answered his critics by establishing himself among the game's elite hitters in his rookie season. He was also considered among the top outfielders, with a strong and very accurate throwing arm.

Born on Oct. 22, 1973, in Kasugai, Japan, Suzuki was drafted by the Orix Blue Wave of the Japanese Pacific League after finishing high school. In 1994 he won a starting spot on the team and finished the season with a batting average of .385—the second best in the history of Japanese baseball. He collected 210 hits, a record for one season. Through 2000 he won seven consecutive Pacific League batting titles, posted a career average of .353, and led his team to two pennants.

By this time, Suzuki had begun his quest for stardom in the United States. He spent two weeks in the Seattle Mariners' 1999 spring training camp as part of a U.S.-Japan player exchange. He made his major league

debut with the Mariners in 2001 and went on to have a stellar season, capturing the AL rookie of the year award and a Gold Glove. His batting average in the 2001 regular season was .350, and it was .421 in postseason games. In 2004 Suzuki broke George Sisler's 84-year-old record for most hits in a single season, ending the year with 262 hits and a .372 batting average. He collected more than 200 hits—and was named to the AL All-Star team—in each of his first 10 seasons with the Mariners. His 10 200-hit seasons tied Pete Rose's all-time record and set the mark for most consecutive years in which a player reached the 200-hit plateau.

Ichiro Suzuki, 2010. **Ronald Martinez/Getty Images**

The United States is credited with developing several popular sports, including some—such as baseball, football, and basketball—that, to varying degrees, have been adopted internationally. But baseball, despite the spread of the game throughout the globe and the growing influence of Asian and Latin American leagues and players, is the sport that Americans still recognize as their national pastime. The game has long been woven into the fabric of American life and identity. "It's our game," exclaimed the poet Walt Whitman more than a century ago, "that's the chief fact in connection with it: America's game."

After about the mid–20th century, baseball's claim to being America's game faltered. The sport faced strong competition, not only from football and other professional sports but even more from a massive transition among Americans from public to private, at-home entertainment. Attendance fell at all levels of baseball, and hundreds of semiprofessional and amateur teams folded. In the 1990s, player strikes,

free agency, and the rising cost of attending games added to the woes of major league baseball. Yet, baseball continued to show a remarkable resiliency; by the end of the 20th century, attendance at professional games improved, and attendance at minor league games was close to World War II records. In the early 21st century, baseball still faced serious problems, but the sport was gaining in popularity around the world. A strong case could still be made for baseball holding a special place in the hearts and minds of the American people.

allege To assert without proof or before proving.

bunt To push or tap a baseball lightly with a bat without swinging.

compatriot A person born, residing, or holding citizenship in the same country as another.

franchise A team and its operating organization having membership in a professional sports league.

hallowed Revered.

human growth hormone (HGH) The naturally occurring growth hormone of humans or a genetically engineered form that is used to treat children with growth hormone deficiencies and has been used especially by athletes to increase muscle mass.

indict To charge with a crime by the finding or presentment of a jury (as a grand jury) in due form of law.

integrity Adherence to a code of values; incorruptibility.

merchant marine The personnel operating the privately or publicly owned commercial ships of a nation.

obstruction The act of hindering from passage, action, or operation.

pastime Something that amuses and serves to make time pass agreeably.

perennial Recurring from year to year.

pipestem Resembling the stem of a tobacco pipe; sometimes used to describe a very thin arm or leg.

prolific Marked by abundant productivity.

prominent Widely and popularly known; leading.

prowess Extraordinary ability.

resiliency An ability to recover from or adjust easily to misfortune or change.

revenue The total income produced by a given source.

slur An insulting or disparaging remark or innuendo; aspersion.

stellar Outstanding.

stint A period of time spent at a particular activity.

storied Celebrated in story or history.

tactician One versed in strategy.

transcend To rise above or go beyond the limits of.

vie To strive for superiority; compete.

wild card One picked to fill a leftover tournament or play-off berth after regularly qualifying competitors have all been determined.

Baseball Canada
2212 Gladwin Crescent, Suite A7
Ottawa, ON K1B 5N1
Canada
(613) 748-5606
Web site: http://www.baseball.ca
Baseball Canada is the national governing
    body of baseball in Canada. The site pro-
    vides information on teams and players
    throughout the country as well as the Long
    Term Athlete Development program.

Canadian Baseball Hall of Fame & Museum
P.O. Box 1838
140 Queen Street
St. Marys, ON N4X 1C2
Canada
(519) 284-1838
Web site: http://new.baseballhalloffame.ca
The Canadian Baseball Hall of Fame &
    Museum disseminates information on the
    history of baseball in Canada and offers a
    summer camp designed to promote inter-
    est in the sport among Canada's youth.

Major League Baseball (MLB)
245 Park Avenue
New York, NY 10167
(212) 931-7800

Web site: http://mlb.mlb.com
The Major League Baseball site provides
    information on major league games, play-
    ers, and statistics. Information on its
    Urban Youth Academy is also available.

National Baseball Hall of Fame and Museum
25 Main Street
Cooperstown, NY 13326
(888) HALL-OF-FAME
Web site: http://baseballhall.org
The National Baseball Hall of Fame and
    Museum holds a vast collection of arti-
    facts, photographs, and more chronicling
    the rich history of baseball and its play-
    ers. It also offers various programs and
    events designed to promote interest and
    awareness among the public and youth.

National Collegiate Athletic Association
    (NCAA)
700 W. Washington Street
P.O. Box 6222
Indianapolis, IN 46206
(317) 917-6222
Web site: http://www.ncaa.org
The NCAA site provides information on
    college athletics in the United States and
    addresses issues facing student athletes.

It also offers information on NCAA-sponsored scholarships for students and post graduates.

USA Baseball
403 Blackwell Street
Durham, NC 27701
(919) 474-8721
Web site: http://web.usabaseball.com
USA Baseball is the national governing body of baseball in the United States. The site provides information on men's and women's teams throughout the country as well as the various international competitions in which they compete.

WEB SITES

Due to the changing nature of Internet links, Rosen Educational Services has developed an online list of Web sites related to the subject of this book. This site is updated regularly. Please use this link to access the list:

http://www.rosenlinks.com/spor/base

Angell, Roger. *Five Seasons: A Baseball Companion* (Univ. of Nebraska Press, 2004).

Berman, Len. *The 25 Greatest Baseball Players of All Time* (Sourcebooks, 2010).

Dreier, David. *Baseball: How It Works* (Capstone, 2010).

Edgerton, R.B. *Baseball Around the World* (McFarland, 2005).

Griffel, S.J. *Baseball 101* (Great Source Education Group, 2005).

Kahn, Roger. *The Boys of Summer* (Perennial, 2000).

Nelson, Kadir. *We Are the Ship: The Story of Negro League Baseball* (Hyperion, 2008).

Palmer, Pete, and Gillette, Gary, eds. *The 2005 ESPN Baseball Encyclopedia* (Sterling, 2005).

Stewart, Mark. *Baseball: A History of the National Pastime* (Franklin Watts, 1998).

Wukovits, J.F. *Life in the Negro Baseball Leagues* (Lucent Books, 2005).